Planets are Spheres

Written by
Jill Atkins

This planet is our home.
We are living on this planet.

It is a round shape called a **sphere**.

You can see what it looks like from high up in a rocket.

The blue parts are the seas and the green and brown parts are the land.

Our planet is the third planet from the Sun.

Our planet has air, rivers and lakes. All living things on our planet need these to stay alive.

This cow is drinking from a river.

This dolphin is swimming and leaping in the blue sea.

The Moon is a sphere too.

We can see the Moon at night when the light from the Sun shines on it.

How the Moon looks when you are near it.

The Moon has no air, but people have landed there in their rockets.

Do you think that people will ever start living on the Moon?

As well as our planet, there are seven extra planets. They are all spheres.

They all go around the Sun. We say that they orbit the Sun.

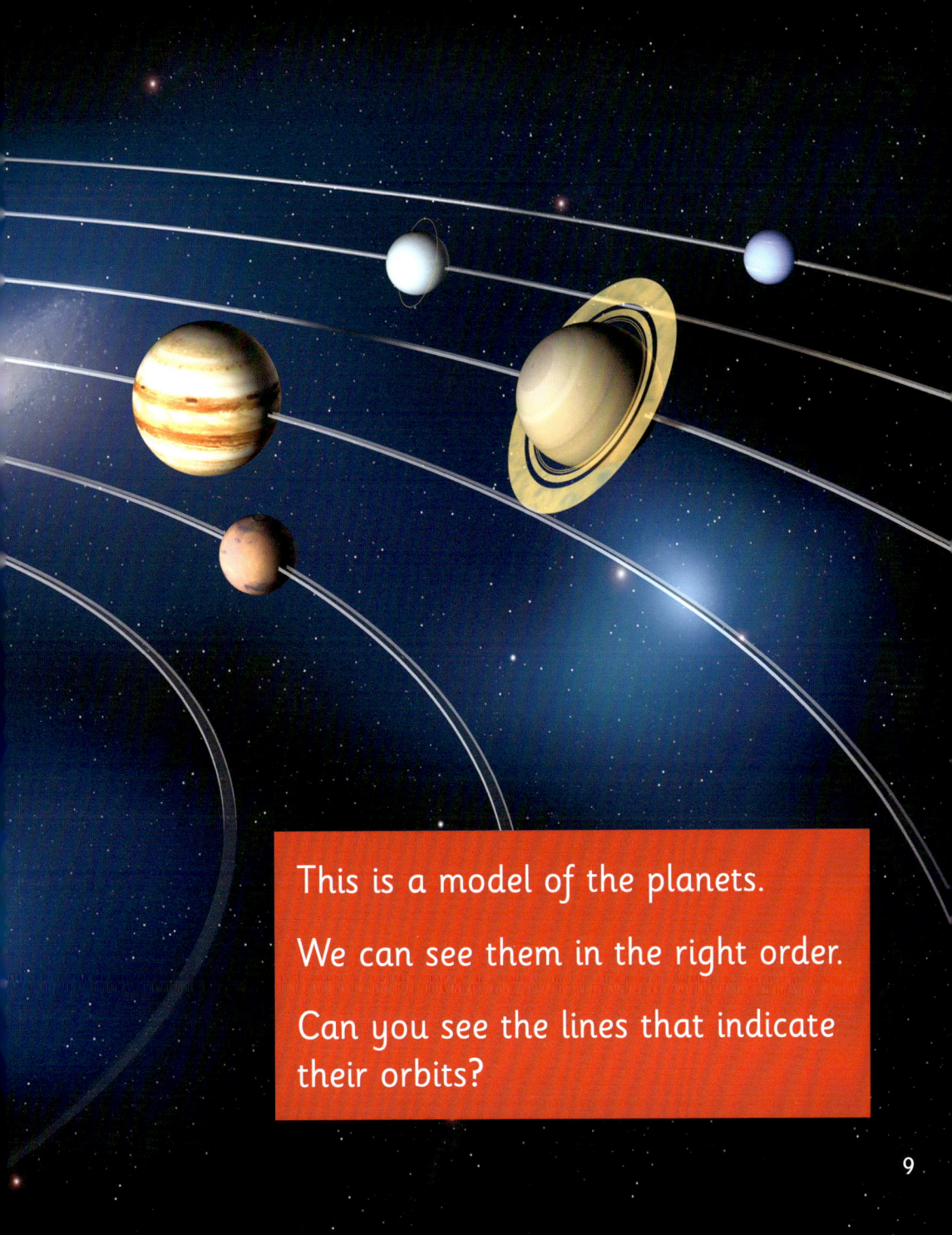

This is a model of the planets.

We can see them in the right order.

Can you see the lines that indicate their orbits?

Mars is one of the planets. It is called the Red Planet.

Sometimes, you can see Mars at night. It shines with a faint red light.

This is how Mars looks if you are standing on it.

People think there are no living things on Mars. The planet has no air to keep people alive.

We have sent rockets to Mars to probe the planet. Do you think they will meet life on Mars?

Saturn is a much bigger planet than Mars, but a lot of Saturn is just made up of gas.

This planet is a sphere too.

Can you see its rings? These rings are made up of little bits of freezing rock.

Saturn is the sixth planet from the Sun and one of the biggest.

It might take several years to reach Saturn in a rocket!

This is the biggest planet.
It has lots of moons too.

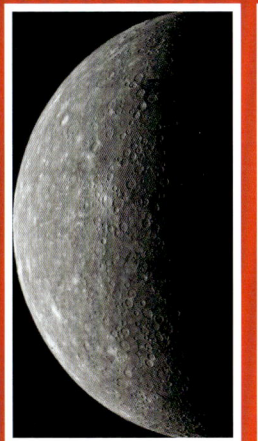 

These planets have no moons.

They are the first and second planets from the Sun.

Neptune is the planet furthest from the Sun.

These girls and boys are looking at a model of the planets.

This boy is painting spheres to make them look like planets.

Do you think the planets are interesting?